The New

U.S. Citizenship Exam

Study Guide - English

2021

128 QUESTIONS YOU NEED TO KNOW

The New

U.S. Citizenship Exam

Study Guide - English

2021

128 QUESTIONS YOU NEED TO KNOW

Jeffrey B. Harris M.Ed

The New U.S. Citizenship Exam Study Guide
-English 2021: 128 Questions You Need to Know

By Jeffrey B. Harris

Copyright © December 2020

Alpharetta, Georgia

Introduction

In order to become a citizen of the United States, there are four tests that you must pass:

1. Speaking Test

2. Reading test

3. Writing test

4. Civics test

Starting December 1st, 2020, there are **128** potential questions that will be asked on the civics portion of the naturalization test. **20** questions are asked, and you must answer **12** correctly. This book is set up to act as a study guide. The first half contains the questions and the second half contains the answers. You should write down the answer in the space provided once you truly know it. Also, new rules state that if you're over 65 years old and have lived in the United States for 20 years or more, then you only need to know the questions marked with a star. Good luck!

Reading Vocabulary Test

People	Abraham Lincoln, George Washington
Civics	American Flag, Bill of Rights, Capital, Citizen, City, Congress, Country, Father of Our Country, Government, President, right, Senators, States, White House
Places	America, United States, U.S.
Holidays	Presidents' Day, Flag Day, Memorial Day, Independence Day, Labor Day, Thanksgiving, Columbus Day
Question Words	How, What, When, Where, Who, Why
Verbs	Can, Come, Do/Does, Elects, Have/has, is/are/was/be, lives/lived, meet, name, pay, vote, want
Other (Function)	A, for, here, in, of, on, the, to, we

Other (Content)	Colors, Dollar Bill, First, Largest, Many, Most, North, One, People, Second, South

Writing Test

People	Adams, Lincoln, Washington
Civics	American Indians, Capital, citizens, Civil War, Congress, Father of our Country, Flag, Free, Freedom of Speech, President, Right, Senators, State(s), White House
Places	Alaska, California, Canada, Delaware, Mexico, New York City, United States, Washington, Washington d.c.

Months	January, February, March, April, May, June, July, August, September, October, November, December
Holidays	Presidents' Day, Flag Day, Memorial Day, Independence Day, Labor Day, Thanksgiving, Columbus Day
Verbs	Can, Come, Do/Does, Elects, Have/has, is/are/was/be, lives/lived, meet, name, pay, vote, want
Other (Functions)	And, During, For, here, in, of, on, the, to, we
Other (Content)	Blue, dollar bill, fifty, first, largest, most, north, one hundred, people, red, second,

	south, taxes, white

Questions

1. What is the form of government of the United States?

2. What is the supreme law of the land?*

3. Name one thing the U.S. Constitution does.

4. The U.S. Constitution starts with the words "We the People." What does "We the People" mean?

5. How are changes made to the U.S. Constitution?

6. What does the Bill of Rights protect?

7. How many amendments does the U.S. Constitution have?*

8. Why is the Declaration of Independence important?

9. What founding document said the American colonies were free from Britain?

10. Name two important ideas from the Declaration of Independence and the U.S. Constitution.

11. The words "Life, Liberty, and the pursuit of Happiness" are in what founding document?

12. What is the economic system of the United States?*

13. What is the rule of law?

14. Many documents influenced the U.S. Constitution. Name one.

15. There are three branches of government. Why?

16. Name the three branches of government.

17. The President of the United States is in charge of which branch of government?

18. What part of the federal government writes laws?

19. What are the two parts of the U.S. Congress?

20. Name one power of the U.S. Congress.*

21. How many U.S. senators are there?

22. How long is a term for a U.S. senator?

23. Who is one of your state's U.S. senators now?

24. How many voting members are in the House of Representatives?

25. How long is a term for a member of the House of Representatives?

26. Why do U.S. representatives serve shorter terms than U.S. senators?

27. How many senators does each state have?

28. Why does each state have two senators?

29. Name your U.S. representative.

30. What is the name of the Speaker of the House of Representatives now?*

31. Who does a U.S. senator represent?

32. Who elects U.S. senators?

33. Who does a member of the House of Representatives represent?

34. Who elects members of the House of Representatives?

35. Some states have more representatives than other states. Why?

36. The President of the United States is elected for how many years?*

37. The President of the United States can serve only two terms. Why?

38. What is the name of the President of the United States now?*

39. What is the name of the Vice President of the United States now?*

40. If the president can no longer serve, who becomes president?

41. Name one power of the president.

42. Who is Commander in Chief of the U.S. military?

43. Who signs bills to become laws?

44. Who vetoes bills?*

45. Who appoints federal judges?

46. The executive branch has many parts. Name one.

47. What does the President's Cabinet do?

48. What are two Cabinet-level positions?

49. Why is the Electoral College important?

50. What is one part of the judicial branch?

51. What does the judicial branch do?

52. What is the highest court in the United States?*

53. How many seats are on the Supreme Court?

54. How many Supreme Court justices are usually needed to decide a case?

55. How long do Supreme Court justices serve?

56. Supreme Court justices serve for life. Why?

57. Who is the Chief Justice of the United States now?

58. Name one power that is only for the federal government.

59. Name one power that is only for the states.

60. What is the purpose of the 10th Amendment?

61. Who is the governor of your state now?*

62. What is the capital of your state?

63. There are four amendments to the U.S. Constitution about who can vote. Describe one of them.

64. Who can vote in federal elections, run for federal office, and serve on a jury in the United States?

65. What are three rights of everyone living in the United States?

66. What do we show loyalty to when we say the Pledge of Allegiance?*

67. Name two promises that new citizens make in the Oath of Allegiance.

68. How can people become United States citizens?

69. What are two examples of civic participation in the United States?

70. What is one way Americans can serve their country?

71. Why is it important to pay federal taxes?

72. It is important for all men age 18 through 25 to register for the Selective Service. Name one reason why.

73. The colonists came to America for many reasons. Name one.

74. Who lived in America before the Europeans arrived?*

75. What group of people was taken and sold as slaves?

76. What war did the Americans fight to win independence from Britain?

77. Name one reason why the Americans declared independence from Britain.

78. Who wrote the Declaration of Independence?*

79. When was the Declaration of Independence adopted?

80. The American Revolution had many important events. Name one.

81. There were 13 original states. Name five.

82. What founding document was written in 1787?

83. The Federalist Papers supported the passage of the U.S. Constitution. Name one of the writers.

84. Why were the Federalist Papers important?

85. Benjamin Franklin is famous for many things. Name one.

86. George Washington is famous for many things. Name one.*

87. Thomas Jefferson is famous for many things. Name one.

88. James Madison is famous for many things. Name one.

89. Alexander Hamilton is famous for many things. Name one.

90. What territory did the United States buy from France in 1803?

91. Name one war fought by the United States in the 1800s.

92. Name the U.S. war between the North and the South.

93. The Civil War had many important events. Name one.

94. Abraham Lincoln is famous for many things. Name one.*

95. What did the Emancipation Proclamation do?

96. What U.S. war ended slavery?

97. What amendment gives citizenship to all persons born in the United States?

98. When did all men get the right to vote?

99. Name one leader of the women's rights movement in the 1800s.

100. Name one war fought by the United States in the 1900s.

101. Why did the United States enter World War I?

102. When did all women get the right to vote?

103. What was the Great Depression?

104. When did the Great Depression start?

105. Who was president during the Great Depression and World War II?

106. Why did the United States enter World War II?

107. Dwight Eisenhower is famous for many things. Name one.

108. Who was the United States' main rival during the Cold War?

109. During the Cold War, what was the main concern of the United States?

110. Why did the United States enter the Korean War?

111. Why did the United States enter the Vietnam War?

112. What did the civil rights movement do?

113. Martin Luther King, Jr. is famous for many things. Name one.*

114. Why did the United States enter the Persian Gulf War?

115. What major event happened on September 11, 2001 in the United States?*

116. Name one U.S. military conflict after the September 11, 2001 attacks.

117. Name one American Indian tribe in the United States.

118. Name one example of an American innovation.

119. What is the capital of the United States?

120. Where is the Statue of Liberty?

121. Why does the flag have 13 stripes?*

122. Why does the flag have 50 stars?

123. What is the name of the national anthem?

124. The Nation's first motto was "E Pluribus Unum." What does that mean?

125. What is Independence Day?

126. Name three national U.S. holidays.*

127. What is Memorial Day?

128. What is Veterans Day?

1. Republic
Constitution-based federal republic
Representative democracy

2.(U.S.) Constitution

3.Forms the government
Defines powers of government
Defines the parts of government
Protects the rights of the people

4.Self-government
Popular sovereignty
Consent of the governed
People should govern themselves
(Example of) social contract

5.Amendments
The amendment process

6.(The basic) rights of Americans
(The basic) rights of people living in the United States

7.Twenty-seven (27)

8.It says America is free from British control.
It says all people are created equal.
It identifies inherent rights.
It identifies individual freedoms.

9.Declaration of Independence

10.Equality
Liberty
Social contract
Natural rights
Limited government
Self-government

11.Declaration of Independence

12.Capitalism
Free market economy

13.Everyone must follow the law.
Leaders must obey the law.
Government must obey the law.
No one is above the law.

14.Declaration of Independence
Articles of Confederation
Federalist Papers
Anti-Federalist Papers
Virginia Declaration of Rights
Fundamental Orders of Connecticut
Mayflower Compact
Iroquois Great Law of Peace

15.So one part does not become too powerful
Checks and balances
Separation of powers

16.Legislative, executive, and judicial
Congress, president, and the courts

17.Executive branch

18.(U.S.) Congress
(U.S. or national) legislature
Legislative branch

19.Senate and House (of Representatives)

20.Writes laws
Declares war
Makes the federal budget

21.One hundred (100)

22.Six (6) years

23.Answers will vary. [District of Columbia residents and
residents of U.S. territories should answer that D.C. (or the
territory where the applicant lives) has no U.S. senators.]

24.Four hundred thirty-five (435)

25.Two (2) years

26.To more closely follow public opinion

27.Two (2)

28.Equal representation (for small states)
The Great Compromise (Connecticut Compromise)

29.Answers will vary.

30. Visit uscis.gov/citizenship/testupdates for the name of the Speaker of the House of Representatives.

31.Citizens of their state

32.Citizens from their state

33.Citizens in their (congressional) district
Citizens in their district

34.Citizens from their (congressional) district

35.(Because of) the state's population
(Because) they have more people
(Because) some states have more people

36.Four (4) years

37.(Because of) the 22nd Amendment
To keep the president from becoming too powerful

38.Visit uscis.gov/citizenship/testupdates for the name of the President of the United States.

39.Visit uscis.gov/citizenship/testupdates for the name of the Vice President of the United States.

40. The Vice President (of the United States)

41.Signs bills into law
Vetoes bills
Enforces laws
Commander in Chief (of the military)
Chief diplomat

42.The President (of the United States)

43.The President (of the United States)

44.The President (of the United States)

45.The President (of the United States)

46.President (of the United States)
Cabinet
Federal departments and agencies

47.Advises the President (of the United States)

48.Attorney General
Secretary of Agriculture
Secretary of Commerce
Secretary of Defense
Secretary of Education
Secretary of Energy
Secretary of Health and Human Services
Secretary of Homeland Security
Secretary of Housing and Urban Development
Secretary of the Interior
Secretary of Labor
Secretary of State
Secretary of Transportation
Secretary of the Treasury
Secretary of Veterans Affairs
Vice President (of the United States)

49.It decides who is elected president.
It provides a compromise between the popular election of the
president and congressional selection.

50.Supreme Court
Federal Courts

51. Reviews laws
Explains laws
Resolves disputes (disagreements) about the law
Decides if a law goes against the (U.S.) Constitution

52. Supreme Court

53. Nine (9)

54. Five (5)

55. (For) life
Lifetime appointment
(Until) retirement

56. To be independent (of politics)
To limit outside (political) influence

57. Visit uscis.gov/citizenship/testupdates for the name of the Chief Justice of the United States.

58. Print paper money
Mint coins
Declare war
Create an army
Make treaties
Set foreign policy

59. Provide schooling and education
Provide protection (police)
Provide safety (fire departments)
Give a driver's license
Approve zoning and land use

60. (It states that the) powers not given to the federal government belong to the states or to the people.

61.Answers will vary. [District of Columbia residents should answer that D.C. does not have a governor.]

62.Answers will vary. [District of Columbia residents should answer that D.C. is not a state and does not have a capital. Residents of U.S. territories should name the capital of the territory.]

63.Citizens eighteen (18) and older (can vote).
You don't have to pay (a poll tax) to vote.
Any citizen can vote. (Women and men can vote.)
A male citizen of any race (can vote).

64.Citizens
Citizens of the United States
U.S. citizens

65.Freedom of expression
Freedom of speech
Freedom of assembly
Freedom to petition the government
Freedom of religion
The right to bear arms

66.The United States
The flag

67.Give up loyalty to other countries
Defend the (U.S.) Constitution
Obey the laws of the United States
Serve in the military (if needed)
Serve (help, do important work for) the nation (if needed)
Be loyal to the United States

68.Naturalize
Derive citizenship
Be born in the United States

69.Vote
Run for office
Join a political party
Help with a campaign
Join a civic group
Join a community group
Give an elected official your opinion (on an issue)
Contact elected officials
Support or oppose an issue or policy
Write to a newspaper

70.Vote
Pay taxes
Obey the law
Serve in the military
Run for office
Work for local, state, or federal government

71.Required by law
All people pay to fund the federal government
Required by the (U.S.) Constitution (16th Amendment)
Civic duty

72.Required by law
Civic duty
Makes the draft fair, if needed

73.Freedom
Political liberty
Religious freedom
Economic opportunity
Escape persecution

74.American Indians
Native Americans

75.Africans
People from Africa

76.American Revolution
The (American) Revolutionary War
War for (American) Independence

77.High taxes
Taxation without representation
British soldiers stayed in Americans' houses (boarding, quartering)
They did not have self-government
Boston Massacre
Boston Tea Party (Tea Act)
Stamp Act
Sugar Act
Townshend Acts
Intolerable (Coercive) Acts

78.(Thomas) Jefferson

79.July 4, 1776

80.(Battle of) Bunker Hill
Declaration of Independence
Washington Crossing the Delaware (Battle of Trenton)
(Battle of) Saratoga
Valley Forge (Encampment)
(Battle of) Yorktown (British surrender at Yorktown)

81.New Hampshire
Massachusetts
Rhode Island
Connecticut
New York
New Jersey

Pennsylvania
Delaware
Maryland
Virginia
North Carolina
South Carolina
Georgia

82.(U.S.) Constitution

83.(James) Madison
(Alexander) Hamilton
(John) Jay
Publius

84.They helped people understand the (U.S.) Constitution.
They supported passing the (U.S.) Constitution.

85.Founded the first free public libraries
First Postmaster General of the United States
Helped write the Declaration of Independence
Inventor
U.S. diplomat

86."Father of Our Country"
First president of the United States
General of the Continental Army
President of the Constitutional Convention

87.Writer of the Declaration of Independence
Third president of the United States
Doubled the size of the United States (Louisiana Purchase)
First Secretary of State
Founded the University of Virginia
Writer of the Virginia Statute on Religious Freedom

88."Father of the Constitution"

Fourth president of the United States
President during the War of 1812
One of the writers of the Federalist Papers

89.First Secretary of the Treasury
One of the writers of the Federalist Papers
Helped establish the First Bank of the United States
Aide to General George Washington
Member of the Continental Congress

90.Louisiana Territory
Louisiana

91.War of 1812
Mexican-American War
Civil War
Spanish-American War

92.The Civil War

93.(Battle of) Fort Sumter
Emancipation Proclamation
(Battle of) Vicksburg
(Battle of) Gettysburg
Sherman's March
(Surrender at) Appomattox
(Battle of) Antietam/Sharpsburg
Lincoln was assassinated.

94.Freed the slaves (Emancipation Proclamation)
Saved (or preserved) the Union
Led the United States during the Civil War
16th president of the United States
Delivered the Gettysburg Address

95.Freed the slaves
Freed slaves in the Confederacy

Freed slaves in the Confederate states
Freed slaves in most Southern states

96. The Civil War

97.14th Amendment

98.After the Civil War
During Reconstruction
(With the) 15th Amendment
1870

99.Susan B. Anthony
Elizabeth Cady Stanton
Sojourner Truth
Harriet Tubman
Lucretia Mott
Lucy Stone

100.World War I
World War II
Korean War
Vietnam War
(Persian) Gulf War

101.Because Germany attacked U.S. (civilian) ships
To support the Allied Powers (England, France, Italy, and
Russia)
To oppose the Central Powers (Germany, Austria-Hungary,
the Ottoman Empire, and Bulgaria)

102.1920
After World War I
(With the) 19th Amendment

103.Longest economic recession in modern history

104.The Great Crash (1929)
Stock market crash of 1929

105.(Franklin) Roosevelt

106.(Bombing of) Pearl Harbor
Japanese attacked Pearl Harbor
To support the Allied Powers (England, France, and Russia)
To oppose the Axis Powers (Germany, Italy, and Japan)

107.General during World War II
President at the end of (during) the Korean War
34th president of the United States
Signed the Federal-Aid Highway Act of 1956 (Created the
Interstate System)

108.Soviet Union
USSR
Russia

109.Communism
Nuclear war

110.To stop the spread of communism

111.To stop the spread of communism

112.Fought to end racial discrimination

113.Fought for civil rights
Worked for equality for all Americans
Worked to ensure that people would "not be judged by the
color of their skin, but by the content of their character"

114.To force the Iraqi military from Kuwait

115.Terrorists attacked the United States
Terrorists took over two planes and crashed them into the World Trade Center in New York City
Terrorists took over a plane and crashed into the Pentagon in Arlington, Virginia
Terrorists took over a plane originally aimed at Washington, D.C., and crashed in a field in Pennsylvania

116.(Global) War on Terror
War in Afghanistan
War in Iraq

117.Apache
Blackfeet
Cayuga
Cherokee
Cheyenne
Chippewa
Choctaw
Creek
Crow
Hopi
Huron
Inupiat
Lakota
Mohawk
Mohegan
Navajo
Oneida
Onondaga
Pueblo
Seminole
Seneca
Shawnee
Sioux
Teton
Tuscarora

118.Light bulb
Automobile (cars, combustible engine)
Skyscrapers
Airplane
Assembly line
Landing on the moon
Integrated circuit (IC)

119.Washington, D.C.

120.New York (Harbor)
Liberty Island [Also acceptable are New Jersey, near New York City, and on the Hudson (River).]

121.(Because there were) 13 original colonies
(Because the stripes) represent the original colonies

122.(Because there is) one star for each state
(Because) each star represents a state
(Because there are) 50 states

123.The Star-Spangled Banner

124.Out of many, one
We all become one

125.A holiday to celebrate U.S. independence (from Britain)
The country's birthday

126.New Year's Day
Martin Luther King, Jr. Day
Presidents Day (Washington's Birthday)
Memorial Day
Independence Day
Labor Day
Columbus Day

Veterans Day
Thanksgiving Day
Christmas Day

127.A holiday to honor soldiers who died in military service

128.A holiday to honor people in the (U.S.) military
A holiday to honor people who have served (in the U.S.
military)

Made in the USA
Las Vegas, NV
11 February 2021